D1605736

A GOLDEN TREASURY OF PSALMS AND PRAYERS

FOR ALL FAITHS

DECORATIONS BY FRITZ KREDEL

THE PETER PAUPER PRESS
Mount Vernon, New York

Note: In the *Golden Treasury of Prayers*,
the source of each prayer is given,
except where the source is un-
known or the prayer is
anonymous

BLESSED is the man that walketh not in
the counsel of the ungodly, nor stand-
eth in the way of sinners, nor sitteth in the
seat of the scornful. But his delight is in the
law of the Lord; and in his law doth he
meditate day and night. And he shall be
like a tree planted by the rivers of water,
that bringeth forth his fruit in his season;
his leaf also shall not wither; and whatso-

ever he doth shall prosper. The ungodly
are not so: but are like the chaff which
the wind driveth away. Therefore the ungodly shall not stand in the judgment, nor
sinners in the congregation of the righteous. For the Lord knoweth the way of the
righteous: but the way of the ungodly
shall perish.   PSALM I

O LORD our Lord, how excellent is thy
name in all the earth! who hast set thy
glory above the heavens. Out of the mouth
of babes and sucklings hast thou ordained
strength because of thine enemies, that
thou mightest still the enemy and the
avenger. When I consider thy heavens,
the work of thy fingers, the moon and the
stars, which thou hast ordained; what is
man, that thou art mindful of him? and
the son of man, that thou visitest him?
For thou hast made him a little lower
than the angels, and hast crowned him
with glory and honor. Thou madest him

to have dominion over the works of thy hands; thou hast put all things under his feet: all sheep and oxen, yea, and the beasts of the field; the fowl of the air, and the fish of the sea, and whatsoever passeth through the paths of the seas. O Lord our Lord, how excellent is thy name in all the earth! PSALM VIII

IN THE LORD put I my trust: how say ye to my soul, Flee as a bird to your mountain? For, lo, the wicked bend their bow, they make ready their arrow upon the string, that they may privily shoot at the upright in heart. If the foundations be destroyed, what can the righteous do? The Lord is in his holy temple, the Lord's throne is in heaven: his eyes behold, his eyelids try, the children of men. The Lord trieth the righteous: but the wicked and him that loveth violence his soul hateth. Upon the wicked he shall rain snares, fire and brimstone, and an horrible tempest: this shall

be the portion of their cup. For the righteous Lord loveth righteousness; his countenance doth behold the upright.

PSALM XI

THE HEAVENS declare the glory of God;
and the firmament sheweth his handy-
work. Day unto day uttereth speech, and
night unto night sheweth knowledge.
There is no speech nor language, where
their voice is not heard. Their line is gone
out through all the earth, and their words
to the end of the world. In them hath he
set a tabernacle for the sun, which is as a
bridegroom coming out of his chamber,
and rejoiceth as a strong man to run a race.
His going forth is from the end of the
heaven, and his circuit unto the ends of it:
and there is nothing hid from the heat
thereof. The law of the Lord is perfect,
converting the soul: the testimony of the
Lord is sure, making wise the simple. The
statutes of the Lord are right, rejoicing the
heart: the commandment of the Lord is

pure, enlightening the eyes. The fear of the Lord is clean, enduring for ever: and judgments of the Lord are true and righteous altogether. More to be desired are they than gold, yea, than much fine gold: sweeter also than honey and the honeycomb. Moreover by them is thy servant warned: and in keeping of them there is great reward. Who can understand his errors? cleanse thou me from secret faults. Keep back thy servant also from presumptuous sins; let them not have dominion over me: then shall I be upright, and I shall be innocent from the great transgression. Let the words of my mouth, and the meditation of my heart, be acceptable in thy sight, O Lord, my strength, and my redeemer. PSALM XIX

THE LORD is my shepherd; I shall not want. He maketh me to lie down in green pastures: he leadeth me beside the still waters. He restoreth my soul: he leadeth

me in the paths of righteousness for his
name's sake. Yea, though I walk through
the valley of the shadow of death, I will
fear no evil: for thou art with me; thy rod
and thy staff they comfort me. Thou pre-
parest a table before me in the presence
of mine enemies: thou anointest my head
with oil; my cup runneth over. Surely
goodness and mercy shall follow me all
the days of my life: and I will dwell in
the house of the Lord for ever.

PSALM XXIII

As the hart panteth after the water
brooks, so panteth my soul after thee, O
God. My soul thirsteth for God, for the
living God: when shall I come and appear
before God? My tears have been my meat
day and night, while they continually say
unto me, Where is thy God? When I remember these things, I pour out my soul
in me: for I had gone with the multitude,
I went with them to the house of God,
with the voice of joy and praise, with a

multitude that kept holyday. Why art
thou cast down, O my soul? and why art
thou disquieted in me? hope thou in God:
for I shall yet praise him for the help of
his countenance. O my God, my soul is
cast down within me: therefore will I remember thee from the land of Jordan, and
of the Hermonites, from the hill Mizar.
Deep calleth unto deep at the noise of thy
water spouts: all thy waves and thy bil-
lows are gone over me. Yet the Lord will
command his lovingkindness in the day-
time, and in the night his song shall be
with me, and my prayer unto the God
of my life. I will say unto God my rock,
Why hast thou forgotten me? why go I
in mourning because of the oppression of
the enemy? As with a sword in my bones,
mine enemies reproach me; while they say
daily unto me, Where is thy God? Why
art thou cast down, O my soul? and why
art thou disquieted within me? hope thou
in God: for I shall yet praise him, who is

the health of my countenance, and my
God.

GOD IS OUR refuge and strength, a very
present help in trouble. Therefore will not
we fear, though the earth be removed,
and though the mountains be carried into
the midst of the sea; though the waters
thereof roar and be troubled, though the
mountains shake with the swelling thereof.
Selah. There is a river, the streams whereof
shall make glad the city of God, the holy
place of the tabernacles of the most High.
God is in the midst of her; she shall not
be moved: God shall help her, and that
right early. The heathen raged, the king-
doms were moved: he uttered his voice,
the earth melted. The Lord of hosts is with
us; the God of Jacob is our refuge. Selah.
Come, behold the works of the Lord, what
desolations he hath made in the earth. He
maketh wars to cease unto the end of the
earth; he breaketh the bow, and cutteth

the spear in sunder; he burneth the chariot
in the fire. Be still, and know that I am
God: I will be exalted among the heathen,
I will be exalted in the earth. The Lord of
hosts is with us; the God of Jacob is our
refuge. Selah.   PSALM XLVI

O GOD, thou art my God; early will I seek
thee: my soul thirsteth for thee, my flesh
longeth for thee in a dry and thirsty land,
where no water is; to see thy power and
thy glory, so as I have seen thee in the
sanctuary. Because thy lovingkindness is
better than life, my lips shall praise thee.
Thus will I bless thee while I live: I will
lift up my hands in thy name. My soul
shall be satisfied as with marrow and fat-
ness; and my mouth shall praise thee with
joyful lips: when I remember thee upon
my bed, and meditate on thee in the night
watches. Because thou hast been my help,
therefore in the shadow of thy wings will
I rejoice. My soul followeth hard after

thee: thy right hand upholdeth me. But those that seek my soul, to destroy it, shall go into the lower parts of the earth. They shall fall by the sword: they shall be a portion for foxes. But the king shall rejoice in God; every one that sweareth by him shall glory: but the mouth of them that speak lies shall be stopped. PSALM LXIII

BLESS THE LORD, O my soul: and all that is within me, bless his holy name. Bless the Lord, O my soul, and forget not all his benefits: Who forgiveth all thine iniquities; Who healeth all thy diseases; Who redeemeth thy life from destruction; Who crowneth thee with lovingkindness and tender mercies; Who satisfieth thy mouth with good things; so that thy youth is renewed like the eagle's. The Lord executeth righteousness and judgment for all that are oppressed. He made known his ways unto Moses, his acts unto the children of Israel. The Lord is merciful and gracious, slow

to anger, and plenteous in mercy. He will
not always chide: neither will he keep his
anger for ever. He hath not dealt with us
after our sins; nor rewarded us according
to our iniquities. For as the heaven is high
above the earth, so great is his mercy
toward them that fear him. As far as the
east is from the west, so far hath he removed our transgressions from us. Like as
a father pitieth his children, so the Lord
pitieth them that fear him. For he knoweth
our frame; he remembereth that we are
dust. As for man, his days are as grass: as
a flower of the field, so he flourisheth. For
the wind passeth over it, and it is gone;
and the place thereof shall know it no
more. But the mercy of the Lord is from
everlasting to everlasting upon them that
fear him, and his righteousness unto children's children; to such as keep his cove-
nant, and to those that remember his
commandments to do them. The Lord
hath prepared his throne in the heavens,

and his kingdom ruleth over all. Bless the Lord, ye his angels, that excel in strength, that do his commandments, hearkening unto the voice of his word. Bless ye the Lord, all ye his hosts; ye ministers of his, that do his pleasure. Bless the Lord, all his works in all places of his dominion: bless the Lord, O my soul. PSALM CIII

MAKE a joyful noise unto the Lord, all ye lands. Serve the Lord with gladness: come before his presence with singing. Know ye that the Lord he is God: it is he that hath made us, and not we ourselves; we are his people, and the sheep of his pasture. Enter into his gates with thanksgiving, and into his courts with praise: be thankful unto him, and bless his name. For the Lord is good; his mercy is everlasting; and his truth endureth to all generations. PSALM C

PRAISE ye the Lord. Blessed is the man that feareth the Lord, that delighteth

greatly in his commandments. His seed shall be mighty upon earth: the generation of the upright shall be blessed. Wealth and riches shall be in his house: and his righteousness endureth for ever. Unto the upright there ariseth light in the darkness: he is gracious, and full of compassion, and righteous. A good man sheweth favor, and lendeth: he will guide his affairs with discretion. Surely he shall not be moved for ever: the righteous shall be in everlasting remembrance. He shall not be afraid of evil tidings: his heart is fixed, trusting in the Lord. His heart is established, he shall not be afraid, until he see his desire upon his enemies. He hath dispersed, he hath given to the poor; his righteousness endureth for ever; his horn shall be exalted with honor. The wicked shall see it, and be grieved; he shall gnash with his teeth, and melt away: the desire of the wicked shall perish.

PSALM CXII

· 17 ·

I will lift up mine eyes unto the hills, from whence cometh my help. My help cometh from the Lord, which made heaven and earth. He will not suffer thy foot to be moved: he that keepeth thee will not slumber. Behold, he that keepeth Israel shall neither slumber nor sleep. The Lord is thy keeper: the Lord is thy shade upon thy right hand. The sun shall not smite thee by day, nor the moon by night. The Lord shall preserve thee from all evil: he shall preserve thy soul. The Lord shall preserve thy going out and thy coming in from this time forth, and even for evermore.

PSALM CXXI

Unto thee lift I up mine eyes, O thou that dwellest in the heavens. Behold, as the eyes of servants look unto the hand of their masters, and as the eyes of a maiden unto the hand of her mistress; so our eyes wait upon the Lord our God, until that he have mercy upon us. Have mercy upon us, O Lord, have mercy upon us: for we

are exceedingly filled with the scorning of
those that are at ease, and with the con-
tempt of the proud.   PSALM CXXIII

EXCEPT THE LORD build the house, they
labor in vain that build it: except the Lord
keep the city, the watchman waketh but
in vain. It is vain for you to rise up early,
to sit up late, to eat the bread of sorrows:
for so he giveth his beloved sleep. Lo,
children are an heritage of the Lord: and
the fruit of the womb is his reward. As
arrows are in the hand of a mighty man;
so are children of the youth. Happy is the
man that hath his quiver full of them: they
shall not be ashamed, but they shall speak
with the enemies in the gate.
            PSALM CXXVII

BLESSED is every one that feareth the
Lord; that walketh in his ways. For thou
shalt eat the labor of thine hands: happy
shalt thou be, and it shall be well with thee.

Thy wife shall be as a fruitful vine by the side of thine house: thy children like olive plants round about thy tables. Behold, that thus shall the man be blessed that feareth the Lord. The Lord shall bless thee out of Zion: and thou shalt see the good of Jerusalem all the days of thy life. Yea, thou shalt see thy children's children, and peace upon Israel. PSALM CXXVIII

OUT OF THE DEPTHS have I cried unto thee, O Lord. Lord, hear my voice: let thine ears be attentive to the voice of my supplications. If thou, Lord, shouldest mark iniquities, O Lord, who shall stand? But there is forgiveness with thee, that thou mayest be feared. I wait for the Lord, my soul doth wait, and in his word do I hope. My soul waiteth for the Lord more than they that watch for the morning: I say, more than they that watch for the morning. Let Israel hope in the Lord: for with the Lord there is mercy, and with him is

plenteous redemption. And he shall re-
deem Israel from all his iniquities.

PSALM CXXX

O GIVE THANKS unto the Lord; for he is
good: for his mercy endureth for ever. O
give thanks unto the God of gods: for his
mercy endureth for ever. O give thanks
to the Lord of lords: for his mercy endureth for ever. To him who alone doeth great
wonders: for his mercy endureth for ever.
To him that by wisdom made the heavens:
for his mercy endureth for ever. To him
that stretched out the earth above the
waters: for his mercy endureth for ever. To
him that made great lights: for his mercy
endureth for ever: the sun to rule by day:
for his mercy endureth for ever: the moon
and stars to rule by night: for his mercy
endureth for ever. To him that smote
Egypt in their firstborn: for his mercy
endureth for ever: and brought out Israel
from among them: for his mercy endureth
for ever: with a strong hand, and with

a stretched out arm: for his mercy endureth for ever. To him which divided the Red sea into parts: for his mercy endureth for ever: and made Israel to pass through the midst of it: for his mercy endureth for ever: but overthrew Pharaoh and his host in the Red sea: for his mercy endureth for ever. To him which led his people through the wilderness: for his mercy endureth for ever. To him which smote great kings: for his mercy endureth for ever: and slew famous kings: for his mercy endureth for ever: Sihon king of the Amorites: for his mercy endureth for ever: and Og the king of Bashan: for his mercy endureth for ever: and gave their land for an heritage: for his mercy endureth for ever: even an heritage unto Israel his servant: for his mercy endureth for ever. Who remembered us in our low estate: for his mercy endureth for ever: and hath redeemed us from our enemies: for his mercy endureth for ever. Who giveth food to all

flesh: for his mercy endureth for ever. O give thanks unto the God of heaven: for his mercy endureth for ever.   PSALM CXXXVI

BY THE RIVERS of Babylon, there we sat down, yea, we wept, when we remembered Zion. We hanged our harps upon the willows in the midst thereof. For there they that carried us away captive required of us a song; and they that wasted us required of us mirth, saying, Sing us one of the songs of Zion. How shall we sing the Lord's song in a strange land? If I forget thee, O Jerusalem, let my right hand forget her cunning. If I do not remember thee, let my tongue cleave to the roof of my mouth; if I prefer not Jerusalem above my chief joy. Remember, O Lord, the children of Edom in the day of Jerusalem; who said, Raze it, raze it, even to the foundation thereof. O daughter of Babylon, who art to be destroyed; happy shall he be, that rewardeth thee as thou hast served

us. Happy shall he be, that taketh and dasheth thy little ones against the stones.

PSALM CXXXVII

Praise ye the Lord. Praise God in his sanctuary: praise him in the firmament of his power. Praise him for his mighty acts: praise him according to his excellent greatness. Praise him with the sound of the trumpet: praise him with the psaltery and harp. Praise him with the timbrel and dance: praise him with stringed instruments and organs. Praise him upon the loud cymbals: praise him upon the high sounding cymbals. Let every thing that hath breath praise the Lord. Praise ye the Lord.

PSALM CL

OUR FATHER, WHO ART IN HEAVEN,
hallowed be Thy name. Thy king-
dom come. Thy will be done on earth, as it
is in heaven. Give us this day our daily
bread. And forgive us our trespasses, as we
forgive those who trespass against us. And
lead us not into temptation; but deliver us
from evil: for Thine is the kingdom, and
the power, and the glory, for ever and ever.
AMEN.

INTO THY HANDS, O God, we commend ourselves, and all who are dear to us, this day. Let the gift of Thy special presence be with us even to its close. Grant us never to lose sight of Thee all the day long, but to worship, and pray to Thee, that at eventide we may again give thanks unto Thee. AMEN. GELASIAN SACRAMENTARY

LORD, make me an instrument of Your peace! Where there is hatred, let me sow love; where there is injury — pardon; where there is doubt — faith; where there is despair — hope; where there is darkness — light: where there is sadness — joy.

O Divine Master, grant that I may not so much seek to be consoled, as to console; to be understood, as to understand; to be loved, as to love; for it is in giving that we receive; it is in pardoning that we are pardoned; it is in dying that we are born to eternal life. FRANCIS OF ASSISI

O God of peace, we turn aside from an unquiet world, seeking rest for our spirits, and light for our thoughts. We bring our work to be sanctified, our wounds to be healed, our sins to be forgiven, our hopes to be renewed, our better selves to be quickened. O Thou, in whom there is harmony, draw us to thyself, and silence the discords of our wasteful lives. Thou in whom all are one, take us out of the loneliness of self, and fill us with the fullness of Thy truth and love. Thou whose greatness is beyond our praise, lift us above our littleness and our daily imperfections; send us visions of the love that is in Thee and of the good that may be in us. Amen.

O Lord Jesus Christ, who art the Way, the Truth, and the Life, we pray Thee suffer us not to stray from Thee, who art the Way, nor to distrust Thee, who art the Truth, nor to rest in any other thing than Thee, who art the Life. Teach us by

Thy Holy Spirit what to believe, what to do, and wherein to take our rest. For Thine own name's sake we ask it. AMEN.

DESIDERIUS ERASMUS

O GOD, keep my tongue from evil and my lips from speaking guile. Be my support when grief silences my voice, and my comfort when woe bends my spirit. Plant humility in my soul, and strengthen my heart with perfect faith in Thee. Help me to be strong in trial and temptation and to be meek when others wrong me, that I may readily forgive them. Guide me by the light of Thy counsel, and let me ever find rest in Thee, who art my Rock and my Redeemer. Let the words of my mouth and the meditation of my heart be acceptable in Thy sight, O Lord, my Rock and my Redeemer. AMEN. UNION PRAYER BOOK

ALMIGHTY GOD, whose light is of Eternity and knoweth no setting, shine forth and be our safeguard through the night;

and though the earth be wrapped in darkness and the heavens be veiled from our sight, let Thy brightness be about our beds, and Thy peace within our souls, and Thy Fatherly blessing upon our sleep this night. AMEN.

O GOD, our Refuge in pain, our Strength in weakness, our Help in trouble, we come to Thee in our hour of need, beseeching Thee to have mercy upon this Thine afflicted servant. O loving Father, relieve his pain. Yet if he needs must suffer, strengthen him, that he may bear his sufferings with patience and as his day is, so may his strength be. Let not his heart be troubled, but shed down upon him the peace which passeth understanding. Though now for a season, if need be, he is in heaviness through his manifold trials, yet comfort him, O Lord, in all his sorrows, and let his mourning be turned into joy, and his sickness into health. AMEN.

O KING OF HEAVEN, where light abounds and life reigns forever, give to our dear ones who are with Thee a full share of Thy treasures, that they may always be white with Thy purity, tranquil with Thy peace, and glad with Thy joy. Let us live warmly in their present love as they live in ours, until the time of separation is past, and we are taken to the land whither they have gone before, there to dwell with them in the perfect love that knows no end. AMEN.

LET ME not seek out of Thee what I can find only in Thee, O Lord, peace and rest and joy and bliss, which abide only in Thine abiding joy. Lift up my soul above the weary round of harassing thoughts to Thy eternal Presence. Lift up my soul to the pure, bright, serene, radiant atmosphere of Thy Presence, that there I may breathe freely, there repose in Thy love, there be at rest from myself, and from all things that weary me; and thence return,

arrayed with Thy peace, to do and bear
what shall please Thee. AMEN.   E. B. PUSEY

GIVE ME, O Lord, a steadfast heart, which
no unworthy affection may drag down-
wards; give me an unconquered heart,
which no tribulation can wear out; give
me an upright heart, which no unworthy
purpose may tempt aside. Bestow upon me
also, O Lord my God, understanding to
know Thee, diligence to seek Thee, wisdom to find Thee, and a faithfulness that
may finally embrace Thee. AMEN.

THOMAS AQUINAS

GRANT UNTO US, Almighty God, the
peace of God that passeth understanding,
that we, amid the storms and troubles of
this our life, may rest in Thee, knowing that
all things are in Thee; not beneath Thine
eye only, but under Thy care, governed by
Thy will, guarded by Thy love, so that
with a quiet heart we may see the storms
of life, the cloud and the thick darkness,

ever rejoicing to know that the darkness
and the light are both alike to Thee. Guide,
guard, and govern us even to the end, that
none of us may fail to lay hold upon the
immortal life. AMEN.   GEORGE DAWSON

FATHER, let me hold Thy hand, and like
a child walk with Thee down all my days,
secure in Thy love and strength. AMEN.

I OFFER UP unto Thee my prayers and in-
tercessions, for those especially who have
in any matter hurt, grieved, or found fault
with me, or who have done me any damage
or displeasure. For all those also whom, at
any time, I may have vexed, troubled,
burdened, and scandalized, by words or
deeds, knowingly or in ignorance; that
Thou wouldst grant us all equally pardon
for our sins, and for our offences against
each other. Take away from our hearts,
O Lord, all suspiciousness, indignation,
wrath, and contention, and whatsoever

may hurt charity, and lessen brotherly love. Have mercy, O Lord, have mercy on those that crave Thy mercy, give peace unto them that stand in need thereof, and make us such as that we may be worthy to enjoy Thy grace, and go forward to life eternal. AMEN.   THOMAS À KEMPIS

O FATHER, light up the small duties of this day's life: may they shine with the beauty of Thy countenance. May we believe that glory may dwell in the commonest task of every day. AMEN.

O THOU full of compassion, I commit and commend myself unto Thee, in whom I am, and live, and know. Be Thou the Goal of my pilgrimage, and my Rest by the way. Let my soul take refuge from the crowding turmoil of worldly thoughts beneath the shadow of Thy wings; let my heart, this sea of restless waves, find peace in Thee, O God. AMEN.   ST. AUGUSTINE

O GOD, who art Peace everlasting, whose chosen reward is the gift of peace, and who hast taught us that the peacemakers are Thy children, pour Thy peace into our souls, that everything discordant may utterly vanish, and all that makes for peace be sweet to us forever. AMEN.

O MOST MERCIFUL GOD, who art both the Mind of Thy creation and the Father of us all, send Thy light to Thy children who grope in mental darkness and the dimness of uncertain sight. Turn the night of their distress into the morning of Thy hope, and cause them and those who watch and wait to rest confidently in Thee. AMEN.

IN THEE, O Lord God, I place my whole hope and refuge; on Thee I rest all my tribulation and anguish; for I find all to be weak and inconstant, whatsoever I behold out of Thee. For many friends cannot profit, nor strong helpers assist, nor the books of the learned afford comfort, nor

any place, however retired and lonely, give shelter, unless Thou Thyself dost assist, strengthen, console, instruct, and guard us. For all things that seem to belong to the attainment of peace and felicity, without Thee, are nothing, and do bring in truth no felicity at all. Thou therefore art the Fountain of all that is good; and to hope in Thee above all things is the strongest comfort of Thy servants. To Thee, therefore, do I lift up mine eyes; in Thee, my God, the Father of mercies, do I put my trust. AMEN. THOMAS À KEMPIS

LORD, I know not what I ought to ask of Thee; Thou only knowest what I need; Thou lovest me better than I know how to love myself. O Father! give to Thy child that which he himself knows not how to ask. I dare not ask either for crosses or consolations: I simply present myself before Thee, I open my heart to Thee. Behold my needs which I know not myself; see

and do according to Thy tender mercy.
Smite, or heal; depress me, or raise me up;
I adore all Thy purposes without knowing
them; I am silent; I offer myself in sacrifice; I yield myself to Thee; I would have
no other desire than to accomplish Thy
will. Teach me to pray. Pray Thyself in
me. AMEN.   FRANÇOIS DE LA MOTHE FÉNELON

AH, LORD OUR GOD, if Thou art so lovely
in Thy creatures, how exceedingly beautiful and ravishing Thou must be in Thyself! AMEN.   HENRY SUSO

O LORD God of our fathers, we bless Thy
holy name, Thy grace and mercy for all
those who have gone before us to rest in
Thee; all, in all vocations, who have
pleased Thee. And, we pray Thee, give us
also grace to walk before Thee as they
walked, in righteousness and self-denial,
that, having labored as they labored, we
may afterwards rest as they rest. AMEN.

CHRISTINA G. ROSSETTI

ALMIGHTY GOD, Lord of all saints and of all souls, look upon us, and so guide and govern us by Thy Spirit that we may come at last to take part with that great host, who, looking back upon the way in which they have been led, praise and magnify Thy holy name. AMEN.   GEORGE DAWSON

O LORD OUR GOD, when the storm is loud, and the night is dark, and the soul is sad and the heart oppressed; then, as weary travelers, may we look to Thee; and beholding the light of Thy love, may it bear us on, until we learn to sing Thy song in the night. AMEN.   GEORGE DAWSON

MAKER AND LOVER OF BEAUTY, we adore Thee for the splendor of the universe. Help us to use its wonders and its loveliness as an open door through which we shall enter into the imperishable beauty of Thy Kingdom; through Him in whose face the full beauty of Thy Being shone. AMEN.

O BLESSED LORD, I beseech Thee to pour down upon me such grace as may not only cleanse this life of mine, but beautify it a little, if it be Thy will, before I go hence and am no more seen. Grant that I may love Thee with all my heart and soul and mind and strength, and my neighbor as myself — and that I may persevere unto the end. AMEN.   JAMES SKINNER

O MOST MERCIFUL REDEEMER, Friend and Brother, may we know Thee more clearly, love Thee more dearly, and follow Thee more nearly; for Thine own sake. AMEN.   RICHARD, BISHOP OF CHICHESTER

O LORD, O Son of Man, who hadst not where to lay Thy head, look in Thy compassion on wandering men and women who have no home. Thou who hadst so little of the comfort of home, be with the outcast and forlorn; Thou who art the living Bread and Water, be present by the wayside at their humble meals; Thou who

didst think upon the straying sheep, remember these lost ones and bring them to
Thy fold. AMEN.

O LORD, our heavenly Father, who order-
est all things for our eternal good, mercifully enlighten our minds, and give us a firm
and abiding trust in Thy love and care.
Silence our murmurings, quiet our fears,
and dispel our doubts, that, rising above
our afflictions and our anxieties, we may rest
on Thee, the Rock of everlasting Strength.
AMEN.   NEW CHURCH BOOK OF WORSHIP

DISMAYED by the strife and jealousy
which are bringing ruin to peoples and
nations, we turn, O Jesus, to Thy most
loving Heart as our only hope. O God of
mercy, with tears we invoke Thee to end
wars and the horror of war. O King of
Peace, we humbly implore the peace for
which we long. From Thy Sacred Heart
Thou didst shed forth over the world di-

vine charity, so that discord might end and
love alone might reign among men. During
Thy life on earth, Thy heart beat with tender compassion for the sorrows of men. In
this day, when hate often dominates, may
Thy divine Heart be once more moved to
pity. Inspire rulers and peoples with coun-
sels of meekness. Heal the discords that
tear nations asunder. Thou who didst shed
Thy precious blood that they might live
as brothers, bring men together once more
in loving harmony. To the cry of the
Apostle Peter: "Save us, Lord, we perish,"
Thou didst answer words of mercy and
didst still the raging waves. Deign now to
hear our trustful prayers and give back to
the world order and peace. And do thou,
O most Holy Virgin, as in other times of
distress, be our help, our protection, and
our safeguard. AMEN.   BENEDICT XV

O GOD, help me to think of Thee in this
bitter trial. Thou knowest how my heart

is rent with grief. In my weakness, tested so severely in soul by this visitation, I cry unto Thee, Father of all life: give me fortitude to say with Thy servant Job: "The Lord hath given; the Lord hath taken away; blessed be the name of the Lord." Forgive the thoughts of my rebellious soul. Pardon me in these first hours of my grief, if I question Thy wisdom and exercise myself in things too high for me. Grant me strength to rise above this trial, to bear with humility life's sorrows and disappointments. Be nigh unto me, O God. Bring consolation and peace to my soul. Praised art Thou, O God, who comfortest the mourners. AMEN.

UNION PRAYER BOOK

TEACH US, good Lord, to serve Thee as Thou deservest; to give and not to count the cost; to fight and not to heed the wounds; to toil and not to seek for rest; to labor and not to ask for any reward, save that of knowing that we do Thy will. AMEN.

IGNATIUS LOYOLA

ALMIGHTY GOD, Lord of the storm and of the calm, the vexed sea and the quiet haven, of day and night, of life and of death; grant unto us so to have our hearts stayed upon Thy faithfulness, Thine unchangingness and love, that, whatsoever betide us, however black the cloud or dark the night, with quiet faith trusting in Thee, we may look upon Thee with untroubled eye, and walking in lowliness towards Thee, and in lovingness towards one another, abide all storms and troubles of this mortal life, beseeching Thee that they may turn to the soul's true good; we ask it for Thy mercy's sake. AMEN.   GEORGE DAWSON

WE SEEM to give him back to Thee, dear God, who gavest him to us. Yet as Thou didst not lose him in giving, so we have not lost him by his return. Not as the world giveth, givest Thou, O Lover of Souls! What Thou givest Thou takest not away. For what is Thine is ours always,

if we are Thine. And life is eternal, and love is immortal, and death is only a horizon, and a horizon is nothing but the limit of our sight. Lift us up, strong Son of God, that we may see further; cleanse our eyes that we may see more clearly; draw us closer to Thyself that we may know ourselves nearer to our beloved who are with Thee. And while Thou dost prepare a place for us, prepare us for that happy place, that where they are, and Thou art, we too may be. AMEN.

WE THANK THEE for the dear and faithful dead, for those who have made the distant heavens a Home for us, and whose truth and beauty are even now in our hearts. One by one Thou dost gather the scattered families out of the earthly light into the heavenly glory, from the distractions and strife and weariness of time to the peace of eternity. We thank Thee for the labors and the joys of these mortal years.

We thank Thee for our deep sense of the mysteries that lie beyond our dust, and for the eye of faith which Thou hast opened for all who believe in Thy Son to outlook that mark. May we live altogether in Thy faith and love, and in that hope which is full of immortality. AMEN. RUFUS ELLIS

O LORD, who art as the shadow of a great rock in a weary land, who beholdest Thy weak creatures, weary of labor, weary of pleasure, weary of hope deferred, weary of self, in Thine abundant compassion and unutterable tenderness, bring us, we pray Thee, unto Thy rest. AMEN.

CHRISTINA G. ROSSETTI

GRANT US, O Lord, to know that which is worth knowing, to praise that which pleaseth Thee most, to esteem that highly which to Thee is precious. Give us the right judgment to discern between things visible and things spiritual, and, above all, to seek after the good pleasure of Thy will. AMEN.

THOMAS À KEMPIS

O Thou who art Love, and who seest all the suffering, injustice and misery which reign in this world; look mercifully upon the poor, the oppressed, and all who are heavy laden with labor and sorrow. Fill our hearts with deep compassion for those who suffer, help us to help them in the hour of their extremity, and hasten the coming of thy blessed kingdom of justice and truth. AMEN.

O Lord, give us all, we beseech Thee, grace and strength to overcome every sin; sins of besetment, deliberation, surprise, negligence, omission; sins against Thee, our self, our neighbor; sins great, small, remembered, forgotten. AMEN.

CHRISTINA G. ROSSETTI

O God, animate us to cheerfulness. May we have a joyful sense of our blessings, learn to look on the bright circumstances of our lot, and maintain a perpetual contentedness under Thy allotments. Fortify our minds against disappointment and

calamity. Preserve us from despondency, from yielding to dejection. Teach us that no evil is intolerable but a guilty conscience; and that nothing can hurt us, if, with true loyalty of affection, we keep Thy commandments, and take refuge in Thee. AMEN. WILLIAM ELLERY CHANNING

O GOD, be merciful to all who groan under the bondage of their sins, and show Thy grace to those who are burdened with the memory of their offenses; that, as not one of us is free from fault, so not one may be shut out from pardon. AMEN.

GELASIAN SACRAMENTARY

WATCH THOU, dear Lord, with those who wake, or watch, or weep tonight, and give Thine angels charge over those who sleep. Tend Thy sick ones, O Lord Christ. Rest Thy weary ones. Bless Thy dying ones. Soothe Thy suffering ones. Pity Thine afflicted ones. Shield Thy joyous ones. And all, for Thy Love's sake. AMEN.

ST. AUGUSTINE

O BLESSED LORD JESUS, give us thankful hearts today for Thee, our choicest gift, our dearest guest. Let not our souls be busy inns that have no room for Thee and Thine, but quiet homes of prayer and praise where Thou mayest find fit company, where the needful cares of life are wisely ordered and put away, and wide, sweet spaces kept for Thee, where holy thoughts pass up and down, and fervent longings watch for and wait Thy coming. So, when Thou comest again, O Blessed One, mayest Thou find all things ready, and Thy servants waiting for no new master, but for one long loved and known. Even so, come, Lord Jesus. AMEN.

GODEFROY RAMBEAU

O LORD, Thou knowest what is best for us; let this or that be done, as Thou shalt please. Give what Thou wilt, and how much Thou wilt, and when Thou wilt. Deal with me as Thou thinkest good, and as best pleaseth Thee. Set me where Thou

wilt, and deal with me in all things just as Thou wilt. Behold, I am Thy servant, prepared for all things; for I desire not to live unto myself, but unto Thee; and Oh, that I could do it worthily and perfectly! AMEN.

THOMAS À KEMPIS

KEEP US THIS NIGHT, O Lord, from all works of darkness, and whether we wake or sleep, let our thoughts and deeds be in accordance with Thy holy will. Preserve us from all dangers and terrors of the night; from restless watching and sorrowful thoughts; from unnecessary or fretful care and imaginary fears. Let us awake tomorrow renewed in strength, and cheerful in spirit; may we arise with holy thoughts, and go forth to live to Thine honor, to the service of our fellowmen, and the comfort and joy of our households. AMEN.

CASPAR NEUMANN

O LORD JESUS CHRIST, Thou Good Shepherd of the sheep, who camest to seek

the lost, and to gather them into Thy fold, have compassion upon those who have wandered from Thee; feed those who hunger, cause the weary to lie down in Thy pastures, bind up those who are broken in heart, and strengthen those who are weak, that we, relying on Thy care and being comforted by Thy love, may abide in Thy guidance to our lives' end. AMEN.

GRANT ME GRACE, O merciful God, to desire ardently all that is pleasing to Thee, to examine it prudently, to acknowledge it truthfully, and to accomplish it perfectly, for the praise and glory of Thy name. AMEN.   THOMAS AQUINAS

O LORD, support us all the day long of this troublous life until the shadows lengthen and the evening comes, and the busy world is hushed, and the fever of life is over, and our work is done. Then in Thy mercy grant us a safe lodging and a holy rest, and peace at the last. AMEN.   CARDINAL NEWMAN

BLESS ME, O God, with the love of Thee, and of my neighbor. Give me peace of conscience, the command of my affections; and for the rest, Thy will be done. O King of peace, keep us in love and charity. AMEN.   THOMAS WILSON

I WILL whatsoever Thou willest; I will because Thou willest; I will in that manner Thou willest; I will as long as Thou willest. AMEN.

O HOLY SPIRIT, Love of God, infuse Thy grace, and descend plentifully into my heart; enlighten the dark corners of this neglected dwelling, and scatter there Thy cheerful beams; dwell in that soul that longs to be Thy temple; water that barren soil, over-run with weeds and briars, and lost for want of cultivating, and make it fruitful with Thy dew from heaven. Oh, come, Thou refreshment of them that languish and faint. Come, Thou Star and Guide of them that sail in the tempestuous

sea of the world, Thou only Haven of the tossed and the shipwrecked. Come, Thou Glory and Crown of the living, and only Safeguard of the dying. Come, Holy Spirit, in much mercy, and make me fit to receive Thee. AMEN. ST. AUGUSTINE

FORGIVE ME, most gracious Lord and Father, if this day I have done or said anything to increase the pain of the world. Pardon the unkind word, the impatient gesture, the hard and selfish deed, the failure to show sympathy and kindly help where I had the opportunity, but missed it; and enable me so to live that I may daily do something to lessen the tide of human sorrow, and add to the sum of human happiness. AMEN. F. B. MEYER

O BLESSED LORD, who didst walk with Thy disciples through the country roads and fields of Galilee, be with Thy messengers every where who go forth in Thy name. Go before them in welcome. Be with them

in fellowship upon the road. And yet as they pass onward, stay Thou behind in the hearts of Thy people; for Thou art the same, and our Friend. AMEN.

LORD, merge my will in Yours. May it accept with love the bitter and sweet of life. Possess my intellect, that I may think of You, aspire to You, be guided by You on my journey through life. No matter how long the years may be, let no murmur escape my lips, no unkind thoughts take shelter in my heart, no self-seeking lurk within my soul. With a smile upon my lips and a song of joy within my heart, may I walk courageously with You, my hidden Lord and Savior. AMEN.

SPEAK, LORD, for Thy servant heareth. Grant us ears to hear, eyes to see, wills to obey, hearts to love; then declare what Thou wilt, reveal what Thou wilt, command what Thou wilt, demand what Thou wilt. AMEN.   CHRISTINA G. ROSSETTI

· 52 ·

HEAR OUR PRAYERS, O Lord, and consider our desires. Give unto us true humility, a meek and quiet spirit, a loving and a friendly, a holy and a useful manner of life; bearing the burdens of our neighbors, denying ourselves, and studying to benefit others, and to please Thee in all things. Grant us to be righteous in performing promises, loving to our relatives; to be gentle and easy to be entreated, slow to anger, and readily prepared for every good work. AMEN.   JEREMY TAYLOR

LORD, without Thee I can do nothing; with Thee I can do all. Help me by Thy grace, that I fall not; help me by Thy strength to resist mightily the very first beginnings of evil, before it takes hold of me; help me to cast myself at once at Thy sacred feet, and lie still there, until the storm be overpast; and, if I lose sight of Thee, bring me back quickly to Thee, and grant me to love Thee better. AMEN.   E. B. PUSEY

LORD, behold our family here assembled. We thank Thee for this place in which we dwell; for the love that unites us; for the peace accorded us this day; for the hope with which we expect the morrow; for the health, the work, the food and the bright skies that make our lives delightful; for our friends in all parts of the earth, and our friendly helpers in this foreign isle.

Give us courage, gaiety and the quiet mind. Spare to us our friends, soften to us our enemies. Bless us, if it may be, in all our innocent endeavors. If it may not, give us the strength to encounter that which is to come, that we be brave in peril, constant in tribulation, temperate in wrath, and in all changes of fortune and down to the gates of death, loyal and loving one to another. AMEN.   ROBERT LOUIS STEVENSON

O LORD, renew our spirits and draw our hearts unto Thyself, that our work may not be to us a burden, but a delight; and

give us such a mighty love to Thee as may sweeten all our obedience. Oh, let us not serve Thee with the spirit of bondage as slaves, but with cheerfulness and the gladness of children, delighting ourselves in Thee, and rejoicing in Thy work. AMEN.

BENJAMIN JENKS

GOD OF OUR LIFE, there are days when the burdens we carry chafe our shoulders and weigh us down; when the road seems dreary and endless, the skies grey and threatening; when our lives have no music in them, and our hearts are lonely, and our souls have lost their courage. Flood the path with light, we beseech Thee; turn our eyes to where the skies are full of promise; tune our hearts to brave music; give us the sense of comradeship with heroes and saints of every age; and so quicken our spirits that we may be able to encourage the souls of all who journey with us on the road of life, to Thy honor and glory. AMEN.

WE BESEECH THEE, our most gracious God, preserve us from the cares of this life, lest we should be too much entangled therein; also from the many necessities of the body, lest we should be ensnared by pleasure; and from whatsoever is an obstacle to the soul, lest, being broken with troubles, we should be overthrown. Give us strength to resist, patience to endure, and constancy to persevere. AMEN.

THOMAS À KEMPIS

MOST GREAT and glorious God, who hast appointed the rivers to hasten with a rapid motion to the sea, be graciously pleased, I most humbly beseech Thee, to make the stream of my will perpetually to flow a cheerful and impetuous course, bearing down pleasure, interest, afflictions, death and all other obstacles and impediments whatsoever before it, till it plunge itself joyfully into the unfathomable ocean of Thy divine will. AMEN.   CHARLES HOW

JESUS, OUR MASTER, do Thou meet us while we walk in the way, and long to reach the Country; so that, following Thy light, we may keep the way of righteousness, and never wander away into the horrible darkness of this world's night, while Thou, who art the Way, the Truth, and the Life, art shining within us. AMEN.

MOZARABIC SACRAMENTARY

LORD, take my lips and speak through them; take my mind, and think through it; take my heart, and set it on fire. AMEN.

W. H. AITKEN

O GOD, by whom the meek are guided in judgment, and light riseth up in darkness for the godly; grant us, in all our doubts and uncertainties, the grace to ask what Thou wouldest have us to do; that the Spirit of wisdom may save us from all false choices, and that in Thy light we may see light, and in Thy straight path may not stumble. AMEN.

WILLIAM BRIGHT

MAKE US, O Lord, to flourish like pure lilies in the courts of Thine house, and to show forth to the faithful the fragrance of good works, and the example of a godly life, through Thy mercy and grace. AMEN.

MOZARABIC SACRAMENTARY

WE REMEMBER all those once known to us on the earth, who have passed into the light of Thy presence. Continue Thy mercy and lovingkindness unto them, we beseech Thee, for evermore. AMEN.

WILLIAM ANGUS KNIGHT

O GOD, the Enlightener of men, who of all graces givest the most abundant blessing upon heavenly love; we beseech Thee to cleanse us from selfishness, and grant us, for Thy love, so to love our brethren that we may be Thy children upon earth; and thereby, walking in Thy truth, attain to Thy unspeakable joy, who art the Giver of life to all who truly love Thee. Grant this prayer, O Lord. AMEN.

ROWLAND WILLIAMS

O God, who tellest the number of the stars, and callest them all by their names; heal, we beseech Thee, the contrite in heart, and gather together the outcasts, and enrich us with the fullness of Thy wisdom. AMEN. SARUM BREVIARY

O make Thy way plain before my face. Support me this day under all the difficulties I shall meet with. I offer myself to Thee, O God, this day, to do in me, and with me, as to Thee seems most meet. AMEN. THOMAS WILSON

O Lord, our heavenly Father, Almighty and everlasting God, who hast safely brought us to the beginning of this day; defend us in the same with Thy mighty power; and grant that this day we fall into no sin, neither run into any kind of danger; but that all our doings, being ordered by Thy governance, may be righteous in Thy sight. AMEN. BOOK OF COMMON PRAYER

ALMIGHTY GOD, comfort us by Thy fullness. Our strength is but weakness, our knowledge is but small, our life but passing away. By Thine eternal wisdom, by Thine unshaken power, Thy constant years, Thine unfailing love, uphold and comfort us, that we, ever feeling that our little lives are altogether in Thee, may look forward to the ending of this mortal life without fear, longing for and hoping for an entrance into that large abundant life where Thou shalt be all in all. AMEN.

GEORGE DAWSON

TAKE, O LORD, and receive my entire liberty, my memory, my understanding, and my whole will. All that I am, all that I have, Thou hast given me, and I will give it back again to Thee to be disposed of according to Thy good pleasure. Give me only Thy love and Thy grace; with Thee I am rich enough, nor do I ask for aught besides. AMEN.

IGNATIUS LOYOLA

O LORD, the Author and Persuader of peace, love, and good-will, soften our hard and steely hearts, warm our icy and frozen hearts, that we may wish well to one another, and may be the true disciples of Jesus Christ. And give us grace even now to begin to show forth that heavenly life, wherein there is no disagreement nor hatred, but peace and love on all hands, one toward another. AMEN.

LUDOVICUS VIVES